Chair Yoga For Weight Loss

Chair Yoga for Weight Loss: Just 10 Minutes a Day for Effortless Weight Loss with Low-Impact Exercises | 28-Day Challenge Designed for Seniors & Beginners (50+ Easy-to-Follow Illustrated Exercises)

Barbara Lewiss

EXCLUSIVE BONUS FOR YOU!

Unlock Your Bonus for Chair Yoga for Weight Loss!

To add more value to your experience and provide you with all the necessary tools for success, we're excited to offer you an **exclusive bonus.**

Video Demonstrations: Access detailed video demonstrations of every exercise featured in this book. These guides are carefully created to help you perform each movement accurately and safely, greatly improving your ability to follow along and benefit from the program.

By purchasing this book, you've gained **FREE lifetime access** to these essential resources. To activate your bonus, just flip to the chapter titled **'YOUR BONUS'** and follow the simple steps provided.

Wishing you great success on your journey!

Best wishes,
Barbara Lewiss

\

Copyright © 2024 by Barbara Lewiss

Table of Contents

Introduction

Discover the Power of Chair Yoga for Sustainable Weight Loss

In a world where the quest for health and wellness takes center stage, Chair Yoga emerges as a beacon of hope, offering a path to sustainable weight loss and improved overall well-being.

This introduction aims to shed light on the transformative power of Chair Yoga, a practice that makes the profound benefits of yoga accessible to everyone, regardless of age, fitness level, or mobility limitations.

Chair Yoga, at its core, is not just about adapting yoga poses to a seated position; it's about embracing a holistic approach to health that integrates the body, mind, and spirit. It offers a gentle yet effective means of shedding excess weight, enhancing flexibility, and building muscle tone—all from the comfort and safety of a chair.

This practice transcends the traditional boundaries of yoga by making it inclusive and adaptable, ensuring that anyone can embark on a journey toward a healthier self without the fear of strain or injury. With Chair Yoga, weight loss becomes not just a physical transformation but a journey of self-discovery and empowerment.

The power of Chair Yoga lies in its simplicity and adaptability. It leverages the principles of traditional yoga—mindful breathing, flexibility exercises, and strength-building poses—in a way that is accessible and enjoyable.

Moreover, Chair Yoga addresses the holistic aspects of weight loss. It recognizes that shedding pounds is not just about burning calories; it's about creating a balance within the body and mind. Through focused breathing exercises, it helps reduce stress, which is often a significant barrier to weight loss. By incorporating mindfulness and meditation, Chair Yoga assists in curbing emotional eating, encouraging healthier eating habits, and fostering a more harmonious relationship with food.

As we delve into this book, we'll explore the myriad ways Chair Yoga can transform your life, offering practical guidance on poses, flows, and routines specifically designed for weight loss. Whether you're new to yoga or looking to adapt your practice to suit your needs better, Chair Yoga opens the door to a world of possibilities, where fitness and well-being are within everyone's reach.

1. Why Chair Yoga?

Unveiling the Science: How Chair Yoga Fuels Weight Loss

Chair yoga isn't just a gentle introduction to yoga; it's a powerful ally in your weight loss journey and a path to better health. Let's dive into how this accessible form of exercise can make a big difference:

When you practice chair yoga, you're doing a lot more than just sitting down and stretching. This form of yoga is great for speeding up your metabolism, which is how your body turns the food and drinks you consume into energy. A faster metabolism can help you manage your weight better.

1. **Boost Your Metabolism**: At its core, chair yoga speeds up your metabolism. This is crucial because your metabolism is all about how your body changes food and drink into energy. By improving digestion and increasing oxygen flow with deep breathing, chair yoga helps your body get more energy from your food and burn fat more efficiently.

But that's not all – chair yoga also helps you deal with stress in a healthy way. When we're stressed, we often turn to comfort foods that are high in calories and sugar. This is because of cortisol, a hormone that makes us crave these kinds of foods. Chair yoga encourages you to focus on the present and relax, which can help lower your stress levels and make it easier for you to choose healthier foods.

Reduce Stress and Emotional Eating:

- **Stress Reduction**: Chair yoga teaches mindfulness and relaxation, directly tackling stress, a common trigger for emotional eating. Stress often leads us to reach for comfort foods packed with calories and sugar, thanks to cortisol, a stress-induced hormone.

- **Mindful Eating**: With a focus on present-moment awareness, chair yoga encourages healthier eating choices, making it easier to stick to a nutritious diet.

Plus, chair yoga is great for building and toning muscles without putting too much strain on your body. The exercises and poses in chair yoga are designed to target specific muscle groups, helping you build lean muscle. More muscle means your body burns more calories, even when you're not working out, which can also help with weight loss.

Build and Tone Muscles Without Strain:

- **Gentle on the Body**: Unlike high-impact workouts, chair yoga offers a strain-free method to tone your muscles.

- **Lean Muscle Mass**: By engaging in targeted poses and movements, you'll build lean muscle, which burns more calories than fat, even when you're at rest. This can lead to an increase in your body's resting metabolic rate and aid in weight loss.

In essence, chair yoga offers a **holistic approach** to weight loss. It's not just about burning calories; it's about creating a balanced lifestyle that includes physical health, mental well-being, and mindful nutrition. This makes chair yoga an invaluable part of your journey to a healthier, more balanced you.

Addressing Common Concerns and Misconceptions

Addressing common concerns and misconceptions surrounding chair yoga can clarify its effectiveness and broaden its appeal. Here are some frequently raised questions and the truths that dispel these doubts:

Is chair yoga too easy to provide real fitness benefits?
Contrary to the belief that chair yoga is overly simplistic or just for beginners, this practice offers scalable intensity to challenge individuals at any fitness level. Through focused movements, deep stretches, and strength-building exercises, chair yoga engages the whole body.

Can chair yoga actually contribute to weight loss?
Many wonder if a seated exercise can significantly impact weight loss. Chair yoga not only promotes weight loss through increased muscle activity and metabolic enhancement but also addresses the psychological aspects of eating and stress management. These factors play crucial roles in weight management, making chair yoga an effective tool for those looking to lose weight mindfully.

Is chair yoga only for seniors or those with limited mobility?
While chair yoga is indeed beneficial for seniors and individuals with mobility challenges, it's not exclusively for them. Office workers, people who spend long hours driving, or anyone looking to incorporate more movement into their day can benefit from chair yoga. Its adaptability makes it suitable for a broad audience, offering a convenient way to maintain fitness and relieve stress.

Do I need special equipment for chair yoga?
One of the beauties of chair yoga is its minimal need for equipment. A sturdy chair without wheels is typically all that's required, making it an accessible practice for everyone.

Will chair yoga help with stress and anxiety?
Absolutely. Chair yoga incorporates mindful breathing and meditation techniques, which are proven to reduce stress and anxiety levels. These practices encourage a state of relaxation and present-moment awareness, contributing to emotional and mental well-being alongside physical health.

By addressing these concerns and misconceptions, it becomes clear that chair yoga is a comprehensive, accessible, and effective practice for achieving fitness goals, including weight loss, improving mental health, and enhancing overall quality of life.

2. The Fundamentals of Chair Yoga

Understanding Your Body: Alignment and Posture Basics

Understanding your body is the first step toward a successful chair yoga practice, especially when focusing on alignment and posture basics.

Proper alignment is crucial, not just for the effectiveness of each pose but also for preventing injuries. When seated or performing any yoga pose, your spine should maintain its natural curves, ensuring that your body is aligned over your sit bones, the foundation of your seated posture.

Firstly, become aware of your sitting position. Your feet should be flat on the floor, with knees bent at a 90-degree angle, directly over your ankles.

This positioning helps distribute your weight evenly and supports the natural curve of your spine. Keep your chest open and shoulders rolled back and down, away from your ears, to open up the chest and encourage deep, efficient breathing.

Alignment extends beyond just your spine. Pay attention to your head's position, ensuring it's aligned with your spine, not jutting forward or tilting back.
This reduces strain on your neck and shoulders and facilitates better focus and breathing.

Learning to recognize when your body is properly aligned is a skill that develops with time and practice. It requires mindfulness and body awareness, both of which are enhanced through regular chair yoga practice.
Remember, every body is different, and finding your optimal alignment might require slight adjustments to the poses.

Emphasizing alignment and posture not only improves the physical benefits of chair yoga but also maximizes the flow of energy throughout the body.
This energy, or prana, is vital for maintaining physical and mental well-being, making alignment and posture foundational elements of any yoga practice, including chair yoga.

Breathing Techniques for Maximum Efficiency

Breathing is at the heart of yoga practice, including chair yoga, where specific techniques enhance the efficiency of your practice.

Here are some fundamental breathing techniques used in chair yoga, each serving a unique purpose in enhancing your well-being.

1. **Diaphragmatic Breathing (Belly Breathing):** Sit comfortably with your back straight. Place one hand on your chest and the other on your belly. Inhale slowly through your nose, allowing your belly to expand, while keeping the chest relatively still. Exhale slowly through the mouth or nose, feeling the belly fall. This technique promotes relaxation and stress reduction by activating the parasympathetic nervous system.

2. **Ujjayi Breathing (Ocean Breath):** With your mouth closed, inhale and exhale through your nose while constricting the back of your throat to create a gentle hissing sound on both the inhale and exhale. This method helps maintain focus, heats the body internally, and can aid in maintaining a rhythmic pace during your practice.

3. **Nadi Shodhana (Alternate Nostril Breathing):** This technique involves alternating the breath through each nostril. Start by sitting straight and use your right thumb to close your right nostril. Inhale through the left nostril, then close it with your fingers, and exhale through the right nostril. Inhale through the right nostril, close it, and exhale through the left. This pattern is repeated for several cycles. Nadi Shodhana is known for balancing the body and calming the mind, making it ideal for reducing anxiety and promoting a sense of peace.

4. **Bhramari Breathing (Bee Breath):** Inhale deeply, and as you exhale, make a gentle humming sound with your lips closed and teeth slightly apart. The vibration from the humming can help calm the mind and reduce stress. It's particularly useful for soothing the nervous system and can be a great practice before meditation or sleep.

Each breathing technique offers distinct benefits, from calming the mind to energizing the body. Incorporating these techniques into your chair yoga practice can significantly enhance the effectiveness of the poses by ensuring that you breathe correctly and efficiently. Start with the technique that feels most comfortable and gradually incorporate others to experience their full range of benefits.

Essential Equipment: Selecting the Right Chair and Attire

The beauty of chair yoga lies in its simplicity and accessibility, requiring minimal equipment. Here's a guide to selecting the essential gear for your chair yoga sessions.

Selecting the Right Chair:

1. **Stability:** Opt for a chair without wheels to ensure it remains stationary during your practice. Stability is crucial to prevent slips and maintain poses correctly.

2. **Size:** The chair should allow your feet to rest flat on the floor with your knees at a 90-degree angle. This alignment supports proper posture and balance.

3. **Back Support:** A chair with a straight back encourages upright posture, essential for most chair yoga poses. Avoid overly cushioned chairs, as they can make it difficult to maintain alignment.

4. **Material:** Consider a chair made from a non-slip material or one that you can modify with a yoga mat or towel to prevent sliding while practicing poses.

Selecting the Right Attire:

1. **Comfort and Mobility:** Wear clothing that allows you to move freely without restriction. Flexible materials like cotton or moisture-wicking fabrics keep you comfortable and dry.

2. **Fit:** Choose outfits that fit well—not too tight to restrict movement or too loose to interfere with poses. Proper fitting clothes let you focus on your practice without constant adjustments.

3. **Footwear:** Chair yoga is typically practiced barefoot to enhance stability and connection with the floor. If you prefer wearing something on your feet, opt for yoga socks with grips to prevent slipping.

4. **Layers:** Having an extra layer like a light sweater can be useful for the beginning or end of your session when your body temperature might be lower. You can easily remove it as you warm up.

The Importance of Consistency and Patience

Embarking on the journey of chair yoga requires not just physical engagement but also a commitment to consistency and the cultivation of patience. These two virtues stand as the bedrock of a fruitful yoga practice, guiding you towards sustained progress and deeper self-awareness.

Consistency: The Key to Progress

In chair yoga, as in any form of exercise, consistency is paramount. Regular practice helps in building and maintaining flexibility, strength, and balance, both physically and mentally. It allows the body and mind to familiarize themselves with the poses and breathing techniques, making each session progressively more effective and rewarding.
Aim to integrate chair yoga into your daily routine, even if it's just for a few minutes each day.

Patience: Embracing the Journey

Alongside consistency, patience is a virtue that transforms your chair yoga practice from a mere physical activity into a journey of self-exploration and growth.

The benefits of yoga unfold over time, often subtly and slowly. There might be days when progress seems stagnant or when certain poses feel particularly challenging. It's in these moments that patience becomes your greatest ally. By adopting a patient and non-judgmental attitude towards your practice and your progress, you cultivate a sense of acceptance and gratitude for your body and its capabilities.

Remember, yoga is not a competition, not even with yourself. It's a personal journey that respects your body's pace and its unique needs.
Celebrate the small victories, whether it's noticing a slight improvement in flexibility, experiencing a moment of profound relaxation, or simply committing to your practice on a challenging day.

In essence, chair yoga is a journey that rewards those who approach it with consistency and patience, offering a path to enhanced well-being, deeper mindfulness, and a profound connection with oneself.

3. Chair Yoga Poses for Beginners

Essential Poses: The Heart of Chair Yoga

Starting your chair yoga practice with essential poses is crucial for establishing a solid foundation in yoga. These key exercises are specifically chosen to introduce beginners to the fundamental elements necessary for a comprehensive understanding and execution of yoga, ensuring accessibility while laying the groundwork for more advanced techniques.

By focusing on fundamental poses, you're not just engaging in physical activity but immersing yourself in a practice that combines mental discipline with physical movement. These initial poses are vital for mastering body alignment, breath control, and the attentive execution that yoga demands, providing the bedrock for your journey through more complex sequences and postures.

These foundational exercises offer more than just physical benefits; they embody the intertwining of mental focus and physical strength, leading to improved balance, concentration, and mindfulness. They equip you with the basics of yoga's holistic practice, crucial for anyone aiming to explore deeper aspects of yoga and its transformative power.

Incorporating these primary poses into your routine not only bolsters physical flexibility and strength but also nurtures a sense of inner calm and stability. This approach promotes overall well-being, integrating physical health with mental tranquility. Through diligent practice, you'll find yourself better equipped to handle life's stresses with grace and maintain a balanced perspective in both your personal yoga practice and everyday life.

Let these foundational poses be the pillars upon which you build a resilient, flexible, and deeply personal yoga journey. They are your first steps towards a path of comprehensive wellness, inner harmony, and holistic health, guiding you to unlock the full potential of your yoga practice.

1. Prayer Pose

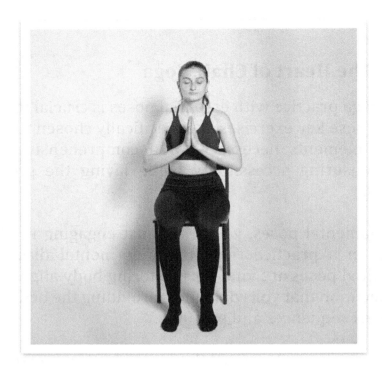

Setup:

1. Begin by sitting comfortably in your chair, ensuring your feet are planted firmly on the ground, hip-width apart.
2. Rest your hands gently on your lap or knees, allowing your shoulders to relax away from your ears.

How To Perform:

1. Bring your palms together in front of your chest in a prayer position, ensuring your elbows are out to the sides.
2. Gently press your palms together while keeping your spine long and tall, engaging your core slightly.
3. Close your eyes, if comfortable, and focus on your breath, inhaling and exhaling slowly and deeply.

Purpose:
The Prayer Pose is designed to center your mind, bring awareness to your body, and prepare you for your yoga practice. It helps in enhancing focus, reducing stress, and cultivating a sense of inner peace.

2. Cat Cow

Setup:

1. Sit at the edge of your chair, placing your feet flat on the ground.
2. Place your hands on your knees or the tops of your thighs.

How To Perform:

1. Inhale, arch your back, and tilt your pelvis back, lifting your chest and chin upward toward the ceiling – this is the Cow position.
2. Exhale, round your spine, tuck your chin to your chest, and pull your belly button towards your spine, rolling your shoulders forward – this is the Cat position.
3. Continue to flow smoothly between Cow and Cat positions with each breath.

Purpose:
This exercise improves spinal flexibility, encourages deep breathing, and helps to relieve tension in the back and neck. It also warms up the body for further poses.

3. Seated Mountain Pose

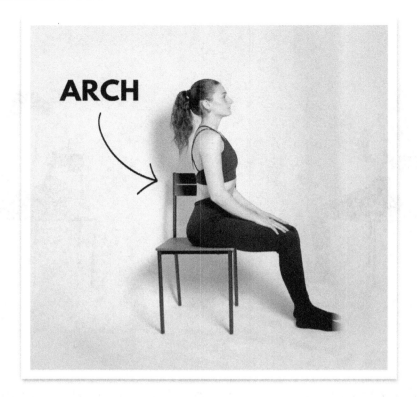

Setup:

1. Sit upright in your chair, feet flat on the ground, and hands resting on your thighs.
2. Draw your shoulders back and down, engaging your core muscles.

How To Perform:

1. Inhale and extend your spine, reaching the crown of your head toward the ceiling.
2. Exhale and ground your feet into the floor, feeling a solid foundation through the soles of your feet and your sit bones.
3. Maintain this posture, taking deep breaths, and focusing on maintaining a strong, tall, and stable position.

Purpose:
Seated Mountain Pose is fundamental in building posture awareness and core strength. It aligns the body correctly, reducing the risk of back pain and improving breathing efficiency.

4. Chair Pigeon Pose

Setup:

1. Sit with your back straight and both feet flat on the ground.
2. Place your right ankle on your left knee, forming a figure-four shape.

How To Perform:

1. Gently press your right knee down towards the floor to increase the stretch.
2. Maintain a straight spine.
3. Hold this position while taking deep breaths, then switch sides.

Purpose:
This pose stretches the hips, glutes, and lower back, improving flexibility and mobility. It's particularly beneficial for those who sit for extended periods.

5. Seated Twist

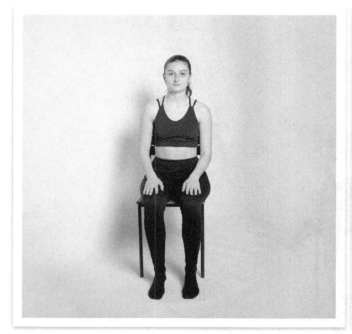 

Setup:

1. Sit upright with your feet flat on the floor.
2. Place your right hand on the back of the chair and your left hand on your right knee.

How To Perform:

1. Inhale and lengthen your spine.
2. Exhale and gently twist your torso to the right, using your hands as leverage to deepen the twist.
3. Hold for a few breaths, then return to center and repeat on the opposite side.

Purpose:
Seated Twist promotes spinal mobility and flexibility. It also aids in digestion and helps relieve tension in the back.

6. Seated Forward Bend

Setup:

1. Begin seated with your feet flat on the ground and your hands resting on your thighs.
2. Inhale and lengthen your spine.

How To Perform:

1. Exhale and hinge at the hips, slowly bending forward, allowing your hands to slide down your legs towards your feet.
2. Relax your neck and allow your head to hang heavy, deepening the stretch in your back.
3. Hold for a few breaths, then inhale as you slowly rise back to a seated position.

Purpose:
This pose stretches the spine and back muscles, promoting flexibility and relieving tension. It also calms the mind and reduces stress.

Flexibility Poses to Enhance Mobility

As we continue our journey into the world of Chair Yoga, it's essential to acknowledge the crucial role flexibility plays in our overall health and well-being.

In the upcoming section, "Flexibility Poses to Enhance Mobility," we delve into a series of carefully selected poses designed not only to improve your range of motion but also to aid in releasing tension throughout the body.
These exercises are meticulously crafted to gently stretch and mobilize various muscle groups, thereby enhancing your flexibility in a safe and supportive manner.

Whether you're looking to alleviate stiffness resulting from prolonged periods of sitting or aiming to improve your overall mobility, these poses offer a path towards achieving your goals.

By dedicating time to these flexibility-enhancing exercises, you can look forward to experiencing a noticeable improvement in how your body moves and feels. Each pose is presented with step-by-step instructions, making it easy for practitioners of all levels to follow along and reap the benefits.

Remember, flexibility is about more than just being able to touch your toes; it's a key component of a balanced and healthy lifestyle. As we explore these poses together, keep an open mind and listen to your body's cues, progressing at a pace that feels right for you. Let's embark on this journey towards enhanced mobility, embracing the transformative power of Chair Yoga to unlock a more flexible, agile, and vibrant version of ourselves.

7. Neck Roll

Setup:

1. Sit comfortably in your chair with your feet flat on the floor and your spine straight.
2. Relax your shoulders down away from your ears and place your hands gently on your lap.

How To Perform:

1. Gently lower your chin to your chest to start the circular motion.
2. Slowly roll your head to the right, bringing your right ear towards your right shoulder.
3. Continue the roll, taking your head back and then bringing your left ear towards your left shoulder. Complete the circle by bringing your chin back to your chest.
4. Repeat the motion in the opposite direction.

Purpose:

The Neck Roll exercise is designed to relieve tension in the neck and shoulders. It promotes flexibility and can help reduce stiffness and pain associated with sitting for prolonged periods.

8. Shoulder Circles

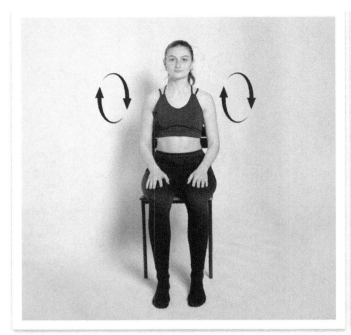 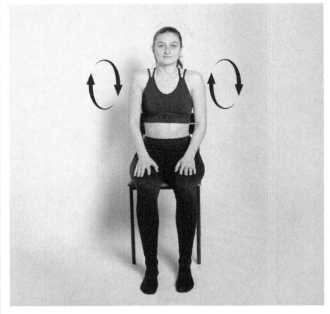

Setup:

1. Sit up straight in your chair, feet flat on the ground and hands resting on your thighs.
2. Ensure your spine is aligned, and your shoulders are relaxed.

How To Perform:

1. Lift your shoulders up towards your ears.
2. Roll them back, drawing big circles with your shoulder blades.
3. Continue rolling them down and then forward, completing the circle.
4. Perform 5 to 10 circles in one direction, then reverse the direction for another 5 to 10 circles.

Purpose:
Shoulder Circles aim to increase the mobility and flexibility of the shoulders and upper back. This exercise helps in relieving tension and tightness, improving posture, and enhancing circulation in the upper body.

\

9. Side Stretch

Setup:

1. Sit upright in your chair with your feet planted firmly on the ground.
2. Keep your spine long and your shoulders relaxed.

How To Perform:

1. Extend your right arm over your head, keeping your elbow straight.
2. Gently lean to the left, stretching the right side of your body.
3. Hold the stretch for a few deep breaths, then return to the starting position.
4. Repeat the stretch on the other side, extending your left arm and leaning to the right.

Purpose:
The Side Stretch focuses on stretching the muscles of the sides of the body, including the obliques, shoulders, and arms. It aids in enhancing lateral mobility, alleviating tightness, and improving overall flexibility and comfort during daily activities.

10. Seated Camel Pose

Setup:

1. Sit at the edge of your chair with your feet flat on the floor, hip-width apart.
2. Place your palms on the back of your pelvis with fingers pointing down.

How To Perform:

1. Gently push your hips forward and arch your back, opening your chest upwards.
2. If comfortable, tilt your head back to deepen the stretch, but do not strain your neck.
3. Hold the pose for a few breaths, feeling the front of your body stretch and open.
4. Carefully return to the starting position.

Purpose:
The Seated Camel Pose aims to stretch the front of the body, particularly the chest, abdomen, and hip flexors. It helps improve spinal flexibility and counteracts the effects of prolonged sitting by encouraging a natural curve in the lower back.

11. Seated Eagle Arms

 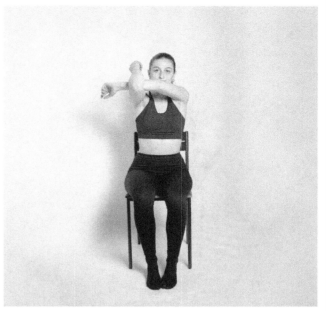

Setup:

1. Sit upright in your chair, feet flat on the ground, and spine straight.
2. Extend your arms parallel to the floor.

How To Perform:

1. Cross your right arm over your left arm at the elbows.
2. Bend your elbows, lifting them while dropping your shoulders down.
3. Try to wrap your forearms around each other and bring your palms to touch, or as close as possible.
4. Hold the pose for several breaths, focusing on the stretch in your shoulders and upper back.
5. Unwind your arms and repeat on the opposite side.

Purpose:
Seated Eagle Arms stretch is designed to relieve shoulder and upper back tension. It enhances flexibility in the shoulder joints, improves arm strength, and encourages better posture.

12. Ankle-to-Knee Pose

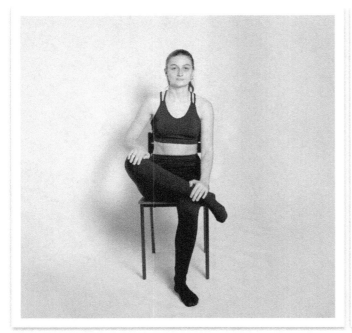 

Setup:

1. Sit firmly in your chair with both feet planted on the ground.
2. Keep your back straight and shoulders relaxed.

How To Perform:

1. Carefully lift your right ankle and place it on your left knee, creating a figure-4 shape with your legs.
2. Gently press down on your right knee to increase the stretch, but do not force it.
3. Lean slightly forward from your hips to deepen the stretch, maintaining a straight back.
4. Hold the pose for several breaths, then switch legs and repeat.

Purpose:
The Ankle-to-Knee Pose focuses on opening the hips and stretching the glutes and outer thighs. It promotes hip mobility, relieves tightness in the lower back, and can help alleviate discomfort associated with sciatica.

4. Advanced Chair Yoga Techniques

Dynamic Poses for Muscle Toning and Sculpting

The journey into Chair Yoga doesn't stop at mastering the basics; it evolves into a more vigorous exploration of dynamic poses designed specifically for muscle toning and sculpting.

As you advance in your practice, you'll encounter exercises that not only deepen your flexibility but also challenge your muscles in new, transformative ways.
These dynamic poses are carefully curated to target key muscle groups, promoting a stronger, more sculpted physique without the need for heavy weights or high-impact activities.

In this chapter, you'll dive into a series of movements that are both accessible from the comfort of your chair and effective in achieving a toned and defined body.

From seated leg lifts that refine thigh and hip muscles to warrior poses that build core and lower body strength, each exercise has been selected to enhance your muscular endurance and aesthetic. These poses will push you beyond the realm of mere flexibility, venturing into the territory where strength meets grace.

By incorporating these dynamic poses into your regular Chair Yoga routine, you'll not only see improvements in muscle tone but also enjoy greater stability and balance. Prepare to engage deeply with each movement, sculpting your body while preserving the mindful essence of yoga practice.

As you progress, remember that the key lies not in the complexity of the pose but in your dedication and consistency. Let's embark on this journey of strength and transformation, one pose at a time.

1. Seated Leg Lifts

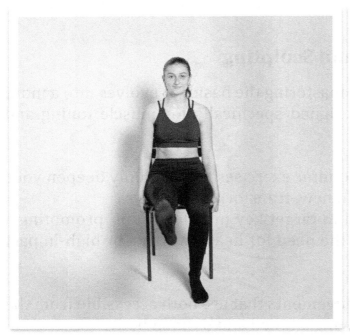 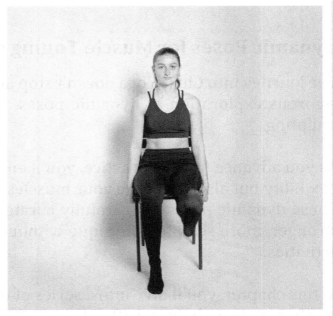

Setup:

1. Sit on the edge of a stable chair with your feet flat on the ground, hip-width apart.
2. Place your hands on the sides of the chair for balance.

How To Perform:

1. Engage your core and straighten your posture.
2. Slowly lift one leg off the ground, keeping it as straight as possible.
3. Raise the leg until it is parallel to the floor or as high as comfortable without compromising your posture.
4. Hold the position for a moment, then slowly lower the leg back to the starting position.
5. Repeat with the other leg.

Purpose:

Seated Leg Lifts target the quadriceps and core muscles, improving lower body strength and stability. This exercise also enhances balance and posture when performed regularly.

\

2. Chair Squats

 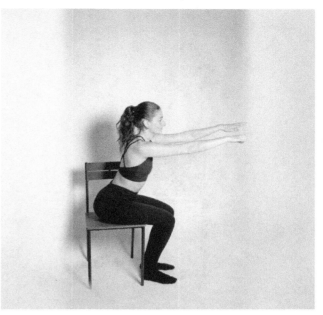

Setup:

1. Stand in front of a chair with your feet hip-width apart.
2. Extend your arms in front of you for balance.

How To Perform:

1. Shift your weight back into your heels as you begin to lower your body towards the chair.
2. Bend your knees and lower yourself until your glutes lightly touch the chair's seat.
3. Ensure your knees are aligned over your toes and do not extend past your feet.
4. Push through your heels to return to a standing position.

Purpose:
Chair Squats focus on strengthening the glutes, quadriceps, and hamstrings. They also improve balance and stability, making them essential for a toned lower body.

3. Calf Raises

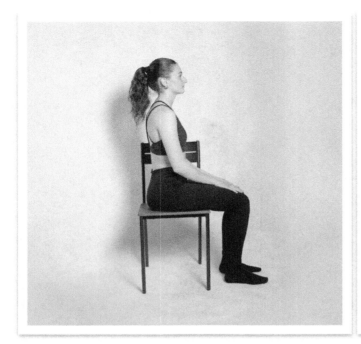 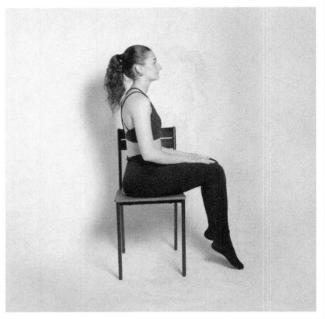

Setup:

1. Sit with your feet flat on the ground, hip-width apart.
2. Hold onto the sides of the chair for support.

How To Perform:

1. Press down through the balls of your feet and lift your heels as high as you can, rising onto your tiptoes.
2. Pause at the top, squeezing your calf muscles.
3. Slowly lower your heels back to the ground.

Purpose:
Calf Raises strengthen the calf muscles and improve ankle stability. They are beneficial for enhancing lower leg definition and supporting posture.

4. Standing Hamstring Curl

Setup:

1. Stand behind the chair, using the backrest for support.
2. Keep your feet hip-width apart and knees slightly bent.

How To Perform:

1. Slowly bend one knee, lifting your heel towards your glutes.
2. Keep the lifted leg aligned with the standing leg as much as possible.
3. Hold the position briefly at the top of the movement.
4. Gently lower the leg back to the starting position.
5. Repeat with the other leg.

Purpose:
The Standing Hamstring Curl targets the hamstrings, improving their strength and flexibility. This exercise also aids in preventing lower back pain and improving balance.

5. Seated Bicycle

Setup:

1. Sit towards the edge of a sturdy chair, maintaining an upright posture.
2. Place your hands behind your head, or cross them over your chest. **(le mani appoggiate alla sedia)**

How To Perform:

1. Lift your knees towards your chest in an alternating motion, simulating a pedaling action.
2. As one knee comes in, extend the other leg out, keeping it elevated off the ground.
3. Rotate your torso slightly towards the knee that is lifted, engaging your core muscles throughout the movement.
4. Continue alternating legs and twisting your torso in a smooth, controlled motion.

Purpose:
The Seated Bicycle exercise targets the abdominal muscles, particularly the obliques, while also engaging the leg muscles. This dynamic movement helps improve core strength, balance, and coordination.

6. Warrior Pose I

Setup:

1. Sit on the edge of the chair with your feet flat on the floor, hip-width apart.
2. Turn your right leg out to the right, keeping your left leg facing forward.

How To Perform:

1. Extend your arms overhead with your palms facing each other, or bring your hands together.
2. Press down through your feet as you lift your chest and gaze upwards, creating a gentle backbend.
3. Bring your arms to chest height and fully extend them in the direction of their respective legs
4. Hold the pose for a few breaths, then return to the starting position and repeat on the other side.

Purpose:
Warrior I helps in strengthening the legs, shoulders, and arms. It also stretches the chest, lungs, and abdomen, promoting better posture and breathing.

7. Seated Side Leg Lift

Setup:

1. Sit on a chair with your feet flat on the floor and hands resting on the seat or your thighs for balance.

How To Perform:

1. Keep one foot on the ground as you slowly lift the other leg to the side as high as comfortably possible without tilting your body.
2. Hold the lift for a moment, engaging the muscles on the outer thigh.
3. Slowly lower the leg back to the starting position.
4. Repeat on the other side.

Purpose:
Seated Side Leg Lift targets the abductor muscles of the outer thigh and hips. This exercise helps improve hip mobility and muscle tone along the side of the body.

8. Seated Star Reach

Setup:

1. Sit with your legs wide apart on the chair, spine straight.
2. Extend your arms out to the sides at shoulder height.

How To Perform:

1. Lean to one side, reaching the opposite hand towards the extended foot.
2. Keep your other arm extended upwards, following the line of your body.
3. Return to the center and then lean to the other side, switching the reach of your arms.
4. Continue alternating sides in a fluid motion.

Purpose:

The Seated Star Reach enhances flexibility across the side body, including the waist, arms, and legs. It also engages the core and improves posture and balance.

Cardiovascular Exercises for Fat Burning

Diving into Chair Yoga lets you chase that great workout feeling, perfect for burning fat and boosting your heart health, without missing out on any of the intensity.

In the next section, titled "Cardio Workouts for Burning Fat," we've put together some great exercises to get your heart beating faster, kick your metabolism into high gear, and burn lots of calories—all while sitting comfortably in your chair.

But it's not just about losing weight.

These workouts are also great for your heart, boosting your energy levels, and adding an exciting spark to your daily routine. Whether you're new to cardio or looking for something new to add to your workouts, these exercises from your chair are a fun mix of challenging and doable.

Get ready to sweat, have fun, and reach a new level of fitness you might not have expected from chair yoga. Every move is carefully planned to give you a complete cardiovascular workout that's not just effective but also fun.

Let's crank up the heat and lay the groundwork for a healthier, more energetic you.

\

9. Seated March

 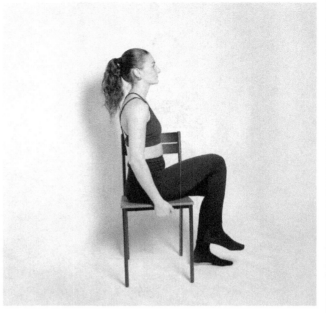

Setup:

1. Sit comfortably on the edge of a sturdy chair with a straight back, feet flat on the floor, and hands resting on your thighs.

How To Perform:

1. Engage your core and sit up tall.
2. Lift your right knee towards your chest as high as comfortably possible while swinging your left arm forward.
3. Lower your right foot back to the floor and simultaneously bring your left arm back.
4. Repeat with the left knee and right arm, mimicking a marching motion.
5. Continue alternating legs and arms in a smooth, controlled march.

Purpose:

The Seated March targets core stability and leg strength while improving cardiovascular endurance. This exercise also boosts circulation and promotes coordination between upper and lower body movements.

10. Seated Kick and Punch

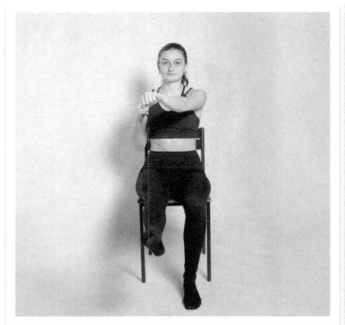 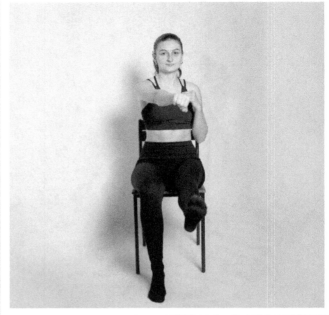

Setup:

1. Begin by sitting on a chair with your back straight, feet planted on the floor, and hands in fists near your chin.

How To Perform:

1. As you extend your right leg forward in a kick, punch forward with your left arm.
2. Bring the right leg and left arm back to the starting position.
3. Alternate by kicking with your left leg and punching with your right arm.
4. Ensure movements are controlled and deliberate, focusing on extending fully and retracting smoothly.

Purpose:

This exercise enhances cardiovascular health by increasing heart rate and engages multiple muscle groups for a comprehensive workout. It also aids in improving balance and coordination.

\

11. Torso Twist

Setup:

1. Sit on the edge of your chair with feet flat on the ground and hands clasped in front of your chest.

How To Perform:

1. Keep your hips facing forward and engage your core.
2. Twist your upper body to the right, aiming to move only from your waist upwards.
3. Return to the center and then twist to the left.
4. Focus on smooth, controlled movements, ensuring your core is engaged throughout the twists.

Purpose:
Torso Twists focus on strengthening the core muscles, particularly the obliques, enhancing spinal flexibility and aiding in digestion. This exercise also provides a mild cardiovascular benefit due to the dynamic movement.

12. Seated Rowing

 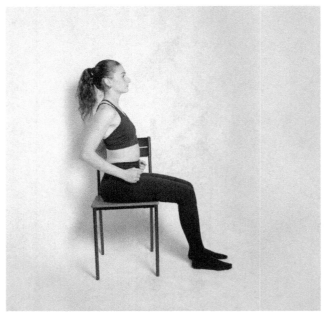

Setup:

1. Sit with legs extended forward slightly and feet planted on the ground. Lean forward at the waist, arms extended forward.

How To Perform:

1. Imagine holding oars; pull your arms back, bending at the elbows and squeezing your shoulder blades together.
2. Extend your arms back out, returning to the starting position.
3. Maintain a straight back throughout the motion, engaging your core to support your movement.

Purpose:

Seated Rowing strengthens the back, shoulders, and arms while providing a cardiovascular workout. This exercise mimics the motion of rowing a boat, engaging multiple muscle groups for an effective full-body exercise.

13. High Knees

Setup:

1. Sit upright on your chair with feet flat on the floor, spaced apart, and hands resting on your thighs.

How To Perform:

1. Lift your right knee as high as you can towards your chest, then place it back down.
2. Repeat with your left knee, creating a high-knee marching motion.
3. Alternate legs quickly, maintaining an upright posture and engaging your core for balance.

Purpose:
High Knees performed while seated focus on engaging the core and strengthening the hip flexors and quadriceps. This exercise also serves as a cardiovascular workout, increasing heart rate and promoting blood flow.

14. Seated Skaters

Setup:

1. Sit on the edge of your chair with legs slightly apart and arms by your sides.

How To Perform:

1. Lean slightly to the right, reaching your left hand towards the right foot while extending your left leg to the side.
2. Quickly switch sides, leaning to the left and reaching your right hand towards the left foot while extending your right leg to the side.
3. Continue alternating sides, mimicking the lateral movements of a speed skater.

Purpose:
Seated Skaters target the obliques, glutes, and thighs, enhancing lateral movement flexibility and strength. This exercise also boosts cardiovascular endurance and promotes coordination.

\

15. Cross Punches

Setup:

1. Sit with a straight back on your chair, feet planted firmly on the ground, and fists held up near your chin.

How To Perform:

1. Punch across your body with your right arm towards the left, rotating your torso with the punch.
2. Retract your right arm and repeat the motion with your left arm, punching across your body towards the right.
3. Continue alternating punches, focusing on engaging your core and rotating your torso with each punch.

Purpose:

Cross Punches strengthen the arms, chest, and core while providing a dynamic cardiovascular workout. This exercise improves coordination and flexibility in the torso, simulating the punching movements found in boxing.

5. Targeted Exercises for Weight Loss

Upper Body Sculpting with Chair Yoga

Starting your adventure with chair yoga is a great way to get more flexible and mindful while also working on making your upper body stronger and more toned.

This part of our guide focuses on exercises for your upper body - like your arms, shoulders, chest, and back. We've picked out yoga poses and movements that are easy to do but really effective.

With chair yoga, you'll see that you don't need heavy weights or lots of equipment to get a strong and toned upper body. Using your own body weight and doing movements with care and focus can really improve how your muscles look, how you stand and move, and how you feel overall.

We've chosen each exercise carefully to make sure you get a workout that's good for your muscles, helps you get stronger, and helps shape your upper body.

If you want to get better at lifting things in your everyday life, add something new to your yoga routine, or just get all the benefits of a good workout, these chair yoga exercises are a safe and effective way to reach your goals.

1. Cactus Arms

Setup:

1. Sit upright on your chair, feet flat on the floor, spine aligned.
2. Raise your arms to the sides, elbows bent at a 90-degree angle, palms facing forward.

How To Perform:

1. Gently press your elbows back, as if trying to touch them behind you, keeping the 90-degree angle.
2. Slowly return to the starting position.

Purpose:
Strengthens the muscles of the upper back and shoulders, promoting better posture and relieving tension in the shoulder area.

2. Seated Reverse Fly

 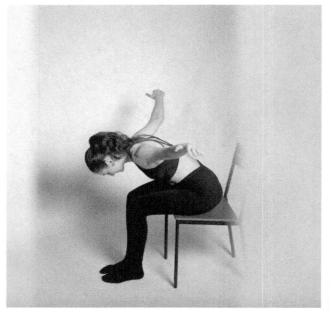

Setup:

1. Sit at the edge of your chair with feet planted firmly on the ground.
2. Lean forward slightly from your hips, keeping your back straight.

How To Perform:

1. Extend your arms down on each side, palms facing each other.
2. Lift your arms to the side, squeezing your shoulder blades together, then lower them back down.

Purpose:
Targets the upper back and rear deltoids, enhancing posture and strengthening muscles that are often neglected.

\

3. Seated Chest Press

Setup:

1. Sit upright on your chair, feet flat and spine straight.
2. Press your palms together in front of your chest.

How To Perform:

1. Push your palms together as firmly as possible, engaging the chest muscles.
2. Hold the press for a few seconds, then release.

Purpose:
Strengthens the chest muscles, contributing to improved upper body strength and better posture.

4. Seated Shoulder Press

 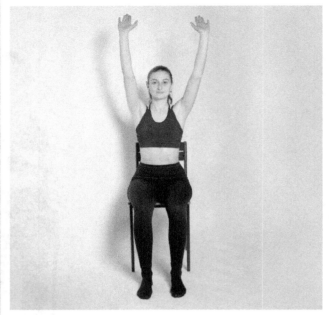

Setup:

1. Sit on the chair with your back straight, feet planted on the ground.
2. Hold your arms out to the sides at shoulder height, elbows bent and palms facing forward.

How To Perform:

1. Extend your arms upwards, pressing towards the ceiling until they are straight.
2. Slowly lower back to the starting position.
3. To make the exercise more difficult, you can hold a pair of lightweight dumbbells or water bottles

Purpose:
Targets the shoulders and upper back, enhancing muscular endurance and strength in the upper body, beneficial for performing daily tasks and improving overall posture.

5. Seated Tricep Dips

Setup:

1. Sit on the edge of your chair, gripping the front of the seat next to your hips with your hands.
2. Bend your legs at a 90-degree angle with your feet firmly planted on the ground.

How To Perform:

1. Move your buttocks off the chair, supported by your arms.
2. Bend your elbows to lower your body towards the ground, then straighten your arms to lift yourself back up.

Purpose:

Strengthens the triceps muscles, improving upper arm definition and assisting in functional movements such as pushing.

6. Butterfly Wings

Setup:

1. Sit upright with your back straight and feet planted on the ground.
2. Bend your elbows, keeping them at shoulder height, and press your palms together in front of your chest.

How To Perform:

1. While keeping your elbows lifted, open your arms out to the sides, stretching the chest.
2. Bring your palms back together in front of your chest.

Purpose:
Targets the chest and shoulder muscles, enhancing flexibility and strength in the upper body, beneficial for improving posture.

7. Uppercuts

Setup:

1. Sit with a straight back, feet flat on the floor.
2. Hold your arms in front of you with elbows bent, palms facing up.

How To Perform:

1. Perform an upward, curving punch with one arm, rotating the torso slightly.
2. Return to the starting position and repeat with the other arm.

Purpose:

Engages the upper arms, shoulders, and core, providing cardiovascular benefits and improving upper body strength and coordination.

8. Arm Circles

Setup:

1. Sit tall on the chair, feet flat on the floor.
2. Extend your arms straight out to the sides at shoulder height.

How To Perform:

1. Rotate your arms in small circles, gradually increasing the size of the circles.
2. Perform for several rotations, then reverse the direction of the circles.

Purpose:
Improves shoulder mobility and strengthens the arm and shoulder muscles, aiding in the prevention of shoulder injuries and tension relief.

9. Chair Warrior II Pose

Setup:

1. Stand beside your chair, holding onto the backrest for support.
2. Step your legs wide apart, turning your right foot out to about 90 degrees and your left foot slightly inwards.

Execution:

1. Extend your arms out to the sides at shoulder height.
2. Bend your right knee, ensuring it is aligned over your right ankle and does not extend beyond your toes, as you gaze over your right hand.
3. Keep your torso centered and your shoulders relaxed.
4. Hold the pose for a few breaths, then gently return to the starting position and repeat on the other side.

Purpose: This pose strengthens the legs, opens the hips and chest, and enhances balance and stability. It is particularly beneficial for improving overall posture and flexibility.

10. Seated Leg Circles

Setup:

1. Sit at the edge of the chair with your spine straight and hands resting on the sides of the chair for support.

How to Perform:

1. Extend one leg straight out in front of you.
2. Begin to draw circles in the air with your extended leg, keeping the movement controlled from the hip joint.
3. Complete several circles in one direction, then switch directions before switching legs.

Purpose:
This exercise enhances hip mobility and strength, engaging the core for stability and improving circulation in the lower limbs.

11. Leg Push-Up

Setup:

1. Sit on the chair with your feet flat on the ground, hip-width apart.

How to Perform:

1. Place your hands on the sides of the chair seat, close to your hips.
2. Using your arms, lift your body slightly off the seat, then extend one leg straight out in front of you.
3. Lower your body back down until your buttocks nearly touches the seat, then push back up.
4. Alternate legs after each push-up.

Purpose:
This exercise targets the triceps, core, and leg muscles, enhancing upper body strength while engaging the core and improving leg flexibility.

High-Intensity Cardio Sessions for Maximum Calorie Burn

High-intensity cardio sessions are a transformative component of any fitness journey, especially when the goal is maximizing calorie burn. In the upcoming pages, we delve into the realm of chair-based high-intensity cardio exercises that are not only accessible but profoundly effective for those seeking substantial weight loss results.

These sessions are designed to elevate your heart rate, enhance your metabolic rate, and incite a significant calorie burn, all from the comfort and safety of a chair.

Whether you're limited by space, mobility, or simply prefer a low-impact approach to fitness, these exercises will challenge you, boost your cardiovascular health, and contribute significantly to your weight loss endeavors.

By incorporating brief, intense bursts of activity followed by short recovery periods, you'll experience the benefits of an elevated afterburn effect, where your body continues to burn calories even after your workout has concluded.

Embrace these high-intensity cardio sessions as a powerful tool in your weight loss arsenal.
Prepare to be amazed at how dynamic and effective seated exercises can be, proving that a chair is not just a place of rest but a gateway to achieving your fitness goals.

Stay tuned as we guide you through each exercise, designed to invigorate your routine and propel you toward your weight loss objectives with clarity, simplicity, and vigor.

12. L and Kick

Setup:

1. Sit up straight on the edge of your chair with your feet flat on the ground.
2. Keep your back straight and your hands on the sides of the chair or on your hips for balance.

How To Perform:

1. Extend your right leg out straight in front of you, parallel to the ground.
2. Simultaneously, extend your left arm out to the side, forming an "L" shape with your body.
3. Return to the starting position and repeat with your left leg and right arm.
4. Continue alternating sides in a smooth, controlled manner.

Purpose:
This exercise engages multiple muscle groups, including your core, legs, and arms, enhancing coordination and balance. It boosts cardiovascular health by increasing heart rate, promoting blood flow, and maximizing calorie burn.

13. Seated Jacks

Setup:

1. Sit at the edge of your chair with your knees together and hands resting beside your body.

How To Perform:

1. Simultaneously open your legs out to the sides and raise your arms above your head, mimicking the motion of a traditional jumping jack.
2. Quickly bring your legs back together and lower your arms to return to the starting position.
3. Repeat the movement in a fast, controlled manner to keep your heart rate up.

Purpose:

Seated Jacks offer a cardio-intensive workout that improves heart health and burns calories. It targets the arms, legs, and core, making it an effective full-body exercise.

14. Arm and Leg Raise

Setup:

1. Sit upright on a chair, feet flat on the ground, and hands resting on your thighs.

How To Perform:

1. Raise your right arm forward and up towards the ceiling while simultaneously lifting your left leg, keeping it straight.
2. Lower your arm and leg back to the starting position.
3. Repeat with your left arm and right leg.
4. Continue alternating sides, maintaining a rhythmic pace.

Purpose:
The Arm and Leg Raise enhances coordination and balance, stimulates the core muscles, and increases cardiovascular endurance. It's a versatile exercise that strengthens both the upper and lower body while contributing to overall calorie expenditure.

15. Seated Speed Bag

Setup:

1. Sit on the edge of your chair, feet flat on the ground, slightly apart for stability.
2. Raise your elbows up to shoulder height, fists in front of your face.

How To Perform:

1. Rotate your fists in small, rapid circles in front of your face, as if hitting a speed bag.
2. Continue the circular motion quickly, engaging your arms and shoulders.
3. Maintain a steady pace, focusing on quick movements for a set duration.

Purpose:
Seated Speed Bag is excellent for improving upper body endurance and coordination. It targets the shoulders, arms, and core, enhancing cardiovascular health and burning calories through high-intensity activity.

16. Chair Mountain Climbers

Setup:

1. Sit on the edge of your chair and lean slightly forward. Place your hands on the sides of the chair for support.

How To Perform:

1. Begin by pushing down on the chair to lift yourself slightly off the seat
2. Lift your right knee towards your chest, then quickly switch by lifting your left knee while lowering the right
3. Continue to alternate knees in a rapid motion, simulating a running or climbing movement
4. Engage your core and maintain a brisk pace for the maximum effect

Purpose:
Chair Mountain Climbers are a seated version of the traditional floor exercise, offering a cardiovascular workout that targets the core, legs, and improves heart rate. This exercise promotes fat burning and enhances stamina.

17. Step Out and Press

Setup:

1. Sit upright with your back straight on the chair, feet flat on the floor, and hands at chest level with elbows bent.

How To Perform:

1. As you step one foot out to the side, simultaneously press your hands forward, extending your arms.
2. Bring the stepped-out foot back to the starting position while pulling your hands back to chest level.
3. Repeat the movement with the other foot, maintaining a rhythmic motion.
4. Focus on the combination of leg stepping and arm pressing for a coordinated movement.

Purpose:
Step Out and Press combines lower and upper body movement to provide a comprehensive workout. It targets the legs, arms, and chest, enhancing cardiovascular fitness and promoting calorie burn. This exercise improves overall body coordination and strength.

\

6. Chair Yoga Flows

Morning Energizer Flow

The Morning Energizer Flow stands as a cornerstone for those seeking an invigorating start to their day.

Within the forthcoming pages, you will be introduced to a series of flows—seamless transitions from one pose to the next, each meticulously designed to awaken your body, boost your energy, and prepare your mind for the day ahead.

Flows, in the context of chair yoga, are more than just a sequence of movements; they are a symphony of stretches, breaths, and poses that, when performed in harmony, amplify the benefits of each individual component.

These flows are specifically tailored to be accessible from the comfort of your chair, ensuring that everyone, regardless of their fitness level or mobility, can partake in this rejuvenating practice.

The Morning Energizer Flow is your gateway to a day filled with clarity, vitality, and a balanced state of mind. It's a gentle yet powerful routine that promises to lift your spirits and energize your body, setting a positive and productive tone for whatever lies ahead.

1. Chair Sun Salutation Flow

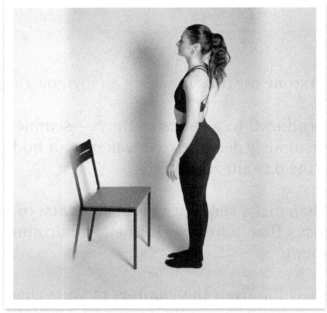 

Setup:

1. Begin by standing in front of the chair, ensuring you have enough space to move freely.

How To Perform:

1. Inhale: Extend your arms overhead, reaching towards the ceiling.

2. Exhale: Hinge at your hips and fold forward, extending your hands towards the chair.
3. Inhale: Lift your torso halfway up, lengthening your spine. Extend your right leg back, preparing for a modified version of the downward-facing dog pose.
4. Exhale: Step your left leg back to join your right, coming into the "Standing Forward Bend Pose."
5. Inhale: Engage your hips to move towards the backrest of the chair, extend your arms forward, and lift your head towards the ceiling, gently arching your back.
6. Exhale: Return to the "Standing Forward Bend Pose," focusing on the transition.
7. Repeat this flow for several rounds, allowing your breath to guide the rhythm of your movements.

Purpose:
The Chair Sun Salutation Flow enhances full-body mobility and flexibility. It effectively warms up the body, synchronizes movement with breath, and serves as an excellent introduction to a yoga practice.

2. Seated Spinal Twist Flow

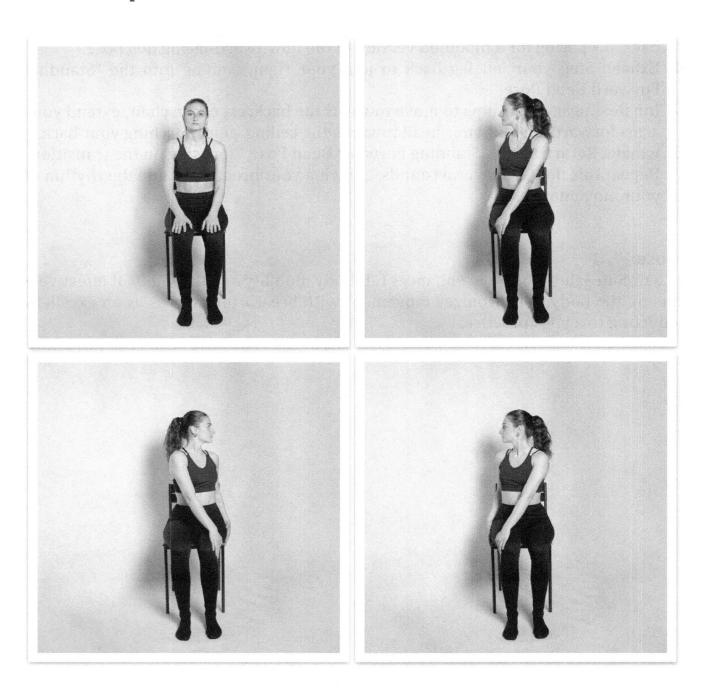

Setup:

1. Begin by sitting comfortably on a chair, ensuring your spine is aligned and feet are flat on the floor, hip-width apart.
2. Place your hands on your thighs or on the armrests of the chair for initial stability.

How To Perform:

1. Inhale deeply, elongating your spine and preparing your body for movement.
2. As you exhale, gently twist your torso to the right, placing your left hand on your right knee and your right hand behind you on the seat of the chair for support.
3. Hold the twist for a few breaths, focusing on deepening the stretch with each exhalation.
4. Inhale as you slowly return to the center, realigning your spine to its initial position.
5. Repeat the twist on the left side, with your right hand on your left knee and your left hand behind you on the chair.
6. Continue alternating sides for several rounds, maintaining smooth and controlled breaths throughout the flow.

Purpose:

The Seated Spinal Twist Flow is designed to enhance spinal flexibility, promote better digestion, and relieve tension in the back and shoulders. This flow encourages a deep engagement with each breath, aiding in the detoxification process and fostering a sense of relaxation and balance within the body. It's an ideal flow for refreshing the mind and improving overall posture, especially beneficial for those spending long hours sitting.

Stress-Relief Evening Routine

The "Stress-Relief Evening Routine" in our Chair Yoga journey is meticulously designed to usher you into a state of tranquility, helping you unwind after a day filled with activities and responsibilities.

This section of our guide focuses on gentle, restorative practices that aim to reduce physical tension, quiet the mind, and prepare your body and spirit for a restful night's sleep.

Within the forthcoming pages, you'll find carefully selected routines that not only ease the stress accumulated throughout the day but also enhance your flexibility and strengthen your body's core, all while seated comfortably in your chair.

These routines are a blend of breathing exercises, gentle stretches, and mindful poses aimed at releasing tightness in key areas known to harbor stress, such as the neck, shoulders, and lower back.

This evening routine is more than just a series of exercises; it's a ritual that invites calmness, centers your thoughts, and reconnects you with your breath, setting the stage for a night of deep, rejuvenating sleep.

Embrace these moments as your personal time to nurture well-being, letting the day's worries dissolve as you flow through each routine. Simple, clear instructions will guide you through each practice, ensuring you gain the maximum benefit from your evening yoga session.

3. Evening Wind-Down Flow

Setup:

1. Choose a quiet, comfortable space where you won't be disturbed.
2. Sit on a chair with your feet flat on the ground and hands resting on your thighs or the armrests. Ensure the chair is stable and supports your back.

How To Perform:

1. **Seated Forward Bend**: Begin with a deep inhale, elongating your spine. As you exhale, hinge at the hips and gently fold forward, allowing your upper body to relax towards your thighs. Let your hands rest on the ground or your feet, wherever they reach comfortably. Hold for a few breaths, feeling the release in your back and neck.

2. **Seated Side Stretch**: Return to an upright position on an inhale. Lift your right arm overhead and lean to the left, stretching the right side of your body. Keep your left hand on your left thigh or the chair for support. Hold for a few breaths, then switch sides.

3. **Seated Twist**: Inhale back to center, and as you exhale, gently twist to the right, placing your left hand on your right knee and your right hand behind you on the chair. Hold for a few breaths, deepening the twist with each exhale, then switch sides.

4. Conclude the flow by returning to a neutral seated position and taking several deep breaths, focusing on exhaling any remaining tension from the day.

Purpose:
The Evening Wind-Down Flow is designed to release physical and mental tension accumulated throughout the day. It encourages relaxation in the muscles, especially those strained from prolonged sitting or standing. By focusing on breathwork and gentle movements, this flow helps to calm the nervous system, preparing your body and mind for a restful evening and a good night's sleep.

4. Mindful Meditation and Breathing Routine

Setup:

1. Sit comfortably on your chair, feet flat on the floor, hands resting on your thighs or knees. Choose a quiet spot where you can meditate undisturbed.
2. Close your eyes gently and take a few deep, natural breaths to center yourself.

How To Perform:

1. Begin with a simple breath awareness exercise. Inhale deeply through your nose, feeling your chest and belly rise, then exhale slowly through your mouth or nose, feeling the body relax. Continue for 2-3 minutes, focusing solely on your breath.

2. Transition to a body scan meditation. Starting from the top of your head, slowly move your attention down through your body, noticing any areas of tension or discomfort. As you exhale, imagine releasing tension from these areas. Continue until you've scanned your entire body.

3. Finish with a gratitude practice. Think of three things you are grateful for today. They can be as simple as enjoying a good meal, having a conversation with a friend, or just the peace of the present moment. Focus on the feeling of gratitude for a few moments.

Purpose:

This Mindful Meditation and Breathing Routine is aimed at reducing stress and enhancing emotional well-being. The breath awareness exercise helps to anchor you in the present moment, alleviating worries about the past or future. The body scan promotes relaxation by identifying and releasing physical tension, while the gratitude practice fosters positive emotions and a sense of contentment. Together, these practices prepare you for a peaceful evening, promoting better sleep and overall well-being.

7. The 28-Day Chair Yoga Weight Loss Challenge

Week-by-Week Guide with Daily Routines

I'm glad you've decided to embark on this transformative journey with the 28-Day Chair Yoga Weight Loss Challenge.

This comprehensive program is meticulously designed to guide you through daily routines, gradually building in intensity and variety to promote sustainable weight loss and overall well-being.

As you progress week by week, you'll explore a blend of core strengthening, flexibility enhancing, muscle toning, and cardiovascular exercises, all achievable from the comfort and safety of your chair.

The challenge is structured to ensure that each day introduces a new set of exercises, allowing your body to adapt and grow stronger without the risk of plateauing. Each week, we focus on different aspects of chair yoga and fitness, ensuring a balanced approach to weight loss that is not only effective but also enjoyable.

Our Week-by-Week Guide provides a clear, day-to-day outline of activities, making it easy to follow and integrate into your daily routine. Whether you're new to chair yoga or looking to deepen your practice, this challenge will offer you the tools and motivation needed to achieve your weight loss goals.

Remember, the key to success in this challenge lies in consistency and patience. Progress might be gradual, but with each day, you're taking a step closer to a healthier, more vibrant you.

Let's embark on this journey together, embracing each day's practice with openness and dedication.

Week 1

Day 1:

Warm Up: Start with a 5-minute seated deep breathing exercise.

Exercise	Page	Sets & Repetitions/Duration
Prayer Pose	16	Hold for 1 minute
Seated Forward Bend	21	3 sets - Hold for 30 seconds
Calf Raises	32	3 sets of 12 repetitions
Seated March	39	3 sets of 1 minute each

Day 2:

Warm Up: Begin with a 5-minute gentle neck and shoulder roll.

Exercise	Page	Sets & Repetitions/Duration
Cat Cow	17	3 sets of 10 repetitions
Chair Pigeon Pose	19	4 sets - Hold each side for 30 seconds
Seated Leg Lifts	30	2 sets of 12 repetitions each leg
Seated Kick and Punch	40	3 sets of 45 seconds per set.

Day 3:

Warm Up:
Start with 5 minutes of seated side stretches to prepare your body.

Exercise	Page	Sets & Repetitions/Duration
Seated Mountain Pose	18	Hold for 1 minute – 2 sets
Side Stretch	25	3 sets - Hold each side for 20 seconds
Standing Hamstring Curl	33	3 sets of 10 repetitions on each leg
Torso Twist	41	3 sets of 45 seconds per set.

\

Day 4:

Warm Up: Begin with 5 minutes of gentle seated twists to warm up your spine and core.

Exercise	Page	Sets & Repetitions/Duration
Seated Twist	20	3 sets - Hold each side for 20 seconds
Neck Roll	23	2 sets of 10 rolls in each direction
Seated Side Leg Lift	36	2 sets of 12 repetitions on each leg
Seated Kick and Punch	40	3 sets of 45 seconds per set

Day 5:

Warm Up: Start with 5 minutes of seated leg lifts to activate your lower body muscles.

Exercise	Page	Sets & Repetitions/Duration
Shoulder Circles	24	3 sets of 10 circles in each direction
Seated Camel Pose	26	3 sets - Hold each side for 20 seconds
Seated Bicycle	34	3 sets of 30 seconds per set
Seated Rowing	42	3 sets of 45 seconds per set

Day 6:

Warm Up: Engage in 5 minutes of deep breathing to oxygenate your body and prepare your mind.

Exercise		Sets & Repetitions/Duration
Seated Eagle Arms	27	3 sets - Hold each side for 20 seconds
Seated Star Reach	37	3 sets of 10 repetitions each side
Seated March	39	2 sets of 1 minute each
Cross Punches	45	3 sets of 1 minute each

Day 7: Rest and Reflect
Take this day to reflect on your progress, practice deep breathing, or a gentle flow like the Seated Spinal Twist Flow to maintain momentum without overexerting.

Week 2

Day 8:

Warm Up: Start with a 5-minute seated deep breathing and gentle upper body stretching to prepare your muscles.

Exercise	Page	Sets & Repetitions/Duration
Warrior Pose I	35	3 sets - Hold each side for 30 seconds
Seated Leg Lifts	30	3 sets of 12 repetitions per leg
Uppercuts	53	3 sets of 15 repetitions
Seated Kick and Punch	40	3 sets of 45 seconds per set

Day 9:

Warm Up: Begin with a 5-minute dynamic stretching focusing on the shoulders and legs to increase blood flow.

Exercise	Page	Sets & Repetitions/Duration
Ankle-to-Knee Pose	28	3 sets - Hold each side for 20 seconds
Seated Side Leg Lift	36	3 sets of 12 repetitions on each leg
Cactus Arms	47	3 sets of 20 repetitions
Seated Skaters	44	3 sets of 45 seconds per set

Day 10:

Warm Up: Spend 5 minutes on gentle seated stretches, focusing on side bends and torso twists to loosen up the body.

Exercise	Page	Sets & Repetitions/Duration
Side Stretch	25	2 sets of 45 seconds per side
Calf Raises	32	3 sets of 15 repetitions
High Knees	43	2 sets of 45 seconds per set
Seated Reverse Fly	48	3 sets of 20 repetitions

\

Day 11:

Warm Up: Begin with a 5-minute breathing exercise, focusing on deep, diaphragmatic breaths to center your mind and body.

Exercise	Page	Sets & Repetitions/Duration
Seated Camel Pose	26	Hold for 30 seconds, repeat 3 times
Standing Hamstring Curl	33	3 sets of 15 repetitions per leg
Seated Chest Press	49	Hold the press for 10 seconds – 5 sets
Seated Speed Bag	62	3 sets of 40 seconds

Day 12:

Warm Up: Initiate your session with 5 minutes of dynamic stretches targeting the arms, legs, and torso to prepare your muscles for the workout ahead

Exercise	Page	Sets & Repetitions/Duration
Seated Forward Bend	21	Hold for 40 seconds, repeat 3 times
Butterfly Wings	52	3 sets of 15 repetitions
Seated Rowing	42	3 sets of 30 seconds
Seated Skaters	44	3 sets of 45 seconds

Day 13:

Warm Up: Spend 5 minutes on seated and standing stretches to increase mobility and prepare your body for the exercises.

Exercise	Page	Sets & Repetitions/Duration
Ankle-to-Knee Pose	28	Hold for 40 seconds per side, repeat twice
Seated Shoulder Press	50	3 sets of 15 repetitions
Arm Circles	54	2 sets of 15 rotations, then reverse the direction of the circles
L and Kick	59	3 sets of 45 seconds

Day 14: Reflect and Light Stretching

Dedicate this day to lighter activities, focusing on gentle stretches like the Seated Spinal Twist Flow and deep breathing exercises to aid recovery and mindfulness.

Week 3

Day 15:

Warm Up: Begin with 5 minutes of gentle seated stretches focusing on the neck, shoulders, and upper back to prepare for upper body exercises.

Exercise	Page	Sets & Repetitions/Duration
Seated Twist	20	Hold for 30 seconds each side, 3 times
Seated Leg Lifts	30	3 sets of 15 repetitions per leg
Seated Kick and Punch	40	3 sets of 30 seconds
High Knees	43	3 sets of 45 seconds

Day 16:

Warm Up: Start with 5 minutes of dynamic stretches, including arm circles and side bends, to warm up the body and increase blood flow to the muscles.

Exercise	Page	Sets & Repetitions/Duration
Chair Warrior II Pose	55	Hold for 30 seconds on each side, 3 sets
Seated Leg Circles	56	3 sets of 12 circles in each direction per leg
Seated Speed Bag	62	3 sets of 30 seconds
Arm and Leg Raise	61	3 sets of 30 seconds

Day 17:

Warm Up: Spend 5 minutes on core activation exercises, such as seated marches and gentle twists, to prepare the body for more intensive work.

Exercise	Page	Sets & Repetitions/Duration
Shoulder Circles	24	4 sets of 15 circles in each direction
Seated Bicycle	34	4 sets of 15 seconds per leg
Leg Push-Up	57	3 sets of 15 repetitions
Seated Jacks	60	3 sets of 30 seconds

Day 18:

Warm Up: Start with 5 minutes of full-body stretching, focusing on side bends and hip rotations to loosen up your lower body and increase flexibility.

Exercise	Page	Sets & Repetitions/Duration
Seated Leg Lifts	30	3 sets of 15 repetitions per leg
Seated Shoulder Press	50	3 sets of 15 repetitions, if possible, add a light weight in your hands
Chair Squats	31	3 sets of 10 repetitions
Step Out and Press	64	4 sets of 15 steps and presses per side

Day 19:

Warm Up: Begin with 5 minutes of gentle stretching, concentrating on the neck, shoulders, and back to prepare for upper body strengthening

Exercise	Page	Sets & Repetitions/Duration
Chair Sun Salutation Flow	66	Follow the flow for 1 minute, 2 sets
Cactus Arms	47	4 sets of 15 repetitions
Seated Tricep Dips	51	3 sets of 10 repetitions
Arm and Leg Raise	61	3 sets of 45 seconds

Day 20:

Warm Up: Start with a 5-minute breathing exercise, followed by gentle arm stretches to wake up the body and focus on core engagement

Exercise	Page	Sets & Repetitions/Duration
Seated Spinal Twist Flow	68	Perform the flow for 3 minutes
Butterfly Wings	52	4 sets of 15 repetitions
Cross Punches	45	4 sets of 45 seconds
Chair Mountain Climbers	63	4 sets of 30 seconds

\

Day 21: Rest and Reflect

Take this day to review your journey, focus on breathing and relaxation techniques, or choose a gentle flow that addresses any personal tension or stiffness

Week 4

Day 22:

Warm-Up: Start with 5 minutes of gentle seated stretching, focusing on the neck, shoulders, and arms to prepare your body.

Exercise	Page	Sets & Repetitions/Duration
Seated Leg Circles	56	3 sets of 15 circles in each direction per leg
Standing Hamstring Curl	33	4 sets of 15 curls per leg
L and Kick	59	3 sets of 30 seconds
Arm and Leg Raise	61	3 sets of 45 seconds

Day 23:

Warm-Up: Spend 5 minutes on cardio warm-up exercises like seated marching or gentle jumping jacks with chair.

Exercise	Page	Sets & Repetitions/Duration
Seated Side Leg Lift	36	3 sets of 15 repetitions per leg
High Knees	43	4 sets of 30 seconds
Seated Reverse Fly	48	4 sets of 15 repetitions
Seated Jacks	60	4 sets of 30 seconds

Day 24:

Warm-Up: Begin with a full-body stretching session, targeting all major muscle groups, for 5 minutes

Exercise	Page	Sets & Repetitions/Duration
Seated Shoulder Press	50	4 sets of 15 repetitions
Chair Squats	31	4 sets of 12 repetitions
Uppercuts	53	4 sets of 12 uppercuts per arm
Step Out and Press	64	4 sets of 30 seconds

Day 25:

Warm-Up: Engage in a 5-minute upper body warm-up with gentle arm swings, shoulder rolls, and wrist circles to prepare your muscles.

Exercise	Page	Sets & Repetitions/Duration
Cactus Arms	47	4 sets of 15 repetitions
Calf Raises	32	4 sets of 20 raises
Seated Speed Bag	62	4 sets of 30 seconds
Leg Push-Up	57	3 sets of 15 repetitions

Day 26:

Warm-Up: Begin with a 5-minute dynamic stretching focusing on the lower body, including hip circles and gentle leg swings

Exercise	Page	Sets & Repetitions/Duration
Arm Circles	54	3 sets of 15 rotations, then reverse the direction of the circles
Seated Skaters	44	3 sets of 30 seconds
High Knees	43	3 sets of 45 seconds
Butterfly Wings	52	4 sets of 20 repetitions

Day 27:

Warm-Up: Spend 5 minutes warming up with full-body movements, such as seated marching and arm raises, to get your blood flowing

Exercise	Page	Sets & Repetitions/Duration
Seated Tricep Dips	51	4 sets of 12 repetitions
Seated Jacks	60	4 sets of 30 seconds
Seated Speed Bag	62	3 sets of 1 minute each
Chair Mountain Climbers	63	3 sets of 1 minute each

Day 28: Celebration and Reflection

On this final day, combine your favorite flows and exercises from the past weeks. Reflect on your progress and celebrate your achievements.

Consider a longer session of Mindful Meditation and Breathing Routine to close your 28-day challenge on a note of gratitude and accomplishment.

Congratulations! You must be super proud of having completed this challenge!

The work doesn't end here! You can repeat the challenge as many times as you wish, incorporating more difficult exercises and/or increasing sets and repetitions.

Remember, all the exercises from the challenge are explained in the **BONUS videos** that come with this book, so don't forget to access the platform! If you haven't done so already, go to the chapter **"YOUR BONUS"** and follow the steps.

Tracking Progress: Tips and Tricks

Tracking your progress throughout the 28-Day Chair Yoga Weight Loss Challenge is not only motivating but also essential for recognizing the changes in your body, flexibility, and overall well-being.

Here are some tips and tricks to effectively monitor your journey and keep the momentum going.

1. Keep a Journal: Documenting your daily workouts, including the exercises you've done, any modifications, and how you felt during and after each session, can be incredibly insightful. Note any progress in flexibility, strength, or endurance, as well as any changes in how you feel mentally and emotionally.

2. Take Photos: A picture is worth a thousand words, and this is especially true for physical transformation. Taking weekly photos in the same position can help you visually track how your body is changing. Remember, progress isn't just about weight loss; it's also about posture, muscle tone, and overall appearance.

3. Set Goals: Beyond the daily exercises, set weekly goals. These could be related to consistency (e.g., not missing a day of practice), intensity (e.g., increasing the number of repetitions), or even mindfulness (e.g., dedicating 5 minutes after each session to meditation). Celebrate when you achieve these goals.

4. Share Your Journey: Whether it's with a friend, family member, or online community, sharing your experience can provide additional motivation and support. It can also make your journey more enjoyable and less isolating.

5. Reflect Weekly: Dedicate time each week to reflect on your progress, challenges, and any adjustments needed to your routine or goals. This reflection can also include acknowledging and celebrating the victories, no matter how small they may seem.

6. Listen to Your Body: As you progress, your body's needs may change. Be open to adjusting your practice to accommodate those needs, whether it means adding new exercises, modifying existing ones, or even incorporating additional rest days.

Note: Remember, progress is personal and can manifest in various ways, from physical changes to improved mental health and increased energy levels. Celebrate all forms of progress and be kind to yourself throughout the process.

8. Nutrition and Chair Yoga

Nutritional Guidelines to Support Your Chair Yoga Journey

Starting your Chair Yoga journey for weight loss isn't just about the physical exercises; it's also about nourishing your body correctly to support your goals. Here's a comprehensive look at nutritional guidelines that can enhance the benefits of your Chair Yoga practice.

1. Balanced Diet: Focus on a balanced diet rich in vegetables, fruits, whole grains, lean proteins, and healthy fats. These foods provide the essential nutrients your body needs for energy, recovery, and overall health. Incorporate a variety of colors in your meals to ensure a wide range of vitamins and minerals.

2. Portion Control: Being mindful of portion sizes can help you avoid overeating. Use smaller plates, bowls, and utensils to help control portions. Listen to your body's hunger and fullness cues to guide how much you eat.

3. Regular Meals: Eating at regular intervals helps regulate your metabolism and keeps energy levels steady throughout the day. Aim for three main meals and one or two healthy snacks to avoid extreme hunger and overeating later.

4. Minimize Processed Foods: Try to limit the intake of processed foods, which are often high in added sugars, unhealthy fats, and sodium. These can contribute to weight gain and detract from your overall health.

5. Healthy Cooking Methods: Choose cooking methods that preserve the nutritional value of food and minimize unhealthy fats. Baking, steaming, grilling, and sautéing are great options compared to frying.

6. Mindful Eating: Pay attention to your food and enjoy each bite. Eating slowly and without distraction allows you to notice when you're full, enjoy your food more, and can help prevent overeating.

7. Hydration: Staying hydrated is crucial for overall health and can aid in weight loss. Water helps to fill you up and can reduce the likelihood of mistaking thirst for hunger.

8. Adapt as Needed: Everyone's body is different, and what works for one person may not work for another. Be open to adjusting your diet based on how your body responds and what feels right for you.

Conclusion

Pairing a mindful, balanced diet with your Chair Yoga routine can significantly enhance your journey toward weight loss and overall wellness. Remember, the goal is to nourish your body, support your practice, and embrace a holistic approach to your health.

Weekly Meal Plan

Here's a simple, balanced meal plan to inspire your week. Remember, adjust portions and options based on your dietary needs and preferences.

Day 1:
- **Breakfast:** Oatmeal with sliced bananas, walnuts, and a drizzle of honey.
- **Lunch:** Quinoa salad with mixed vegetables, chickpeas, and a lemon-tahini dressing.
- **Dinner:** Baked salmon, steamed broccoli, and sweet potato wedges.

Day 2:
- **Breakfast:** Greek yogurt with mixed berries and a sprinkle of granola.
- **Lunch:** Turkey and avocado wrap with whole-grain tortilla and side salad.
- **Dinner:** Stir-fried tofu with mixed vegetables and brown rice.

Day 3:
- **Breakfast:** Smoothie with spinach, banana, almond milk, and a scoop of protein powder.
- **Lunch:** Lentil soup with a slice of whole-grain bread.
- **Dinner:** Grilled chicken breast, quinoa, and grilled asparagus.

Day 4:
- **Breakfast:** Whole grain toast with avocado and poached eggs.
- **Lunch:** Kale Caesar salad with grilled shrimp.
- **Dinner:** Spaghetti squash with marinara sauce and meatballs.

Day 5:
- **Breakfast:** Chia seed pudding made with almond milk and topped with fresh mango.
- **Lunch:** Brown rice sushi rolls with a side of miso soup.
- **Dinner:** Vegetable stir-fry with tofu and a side of jasmine rice.

Day 6:
- **Breakfast:** Scrambled eggs with spinach, mushrooms, and feta cheese.
- **Lunch:** Chicken salad with mixed greens, cucumber, tomatoes, and balsamic vinaigrette.
- **Dinner:** Baked cod with roasted Brussels sprouts and a quinoa salad.

Day 7:

- **Breakfast:** Cottage cheese with pineapple chunks and sliced almonds.
- **Lunch:** Hummus and veggie wrap with whole-grain tortilla.
- **Dinner:** Slow cooker beef stew with multigrain bread.

Snacks (Choose 1-2 per day):
- A handful of nuts.
- Sliced apples with almond butter.
- Carrot sticks with hummus.
- A small bowl of mixed berries.
- Greek yogurt with a drizzle of honey.

Tips for Success:
- Prepare some meals in advance to save time during busy days.
- Stay flexible. If a meal doesn't work out, have a backup plan.
- Listen to your body's hunger cues and adjust portion sizes accordingly.
- Stay hydrated throughout the day, especially before meals.

This meal plan is a guide to help you start integrating more nutritious, balanced meals into your routine. Adjust according to your dietary preferences, restrictions, and nutritional needs

Hydration and Weight Loss: Understanding the Basics

Hydration plays a crucial role in maintaining overall health and can be particularly impactful in your weight loss journey.

Water is essential for metabolizing stored fats and carbohydrates, and proper hydration can enhance your body's ability to burn calories more efficiently.

Here's a breakdown of the basics to help you understand the importance of staying hydrated.

The Role of Hydration in Weight Loss

- **Enhances Metabolism:** Drinking water can temporarily boost your metabolism. Studies show that drinking 17 ounces (about 500 ml) of water can increase metabolic rate by 10-30% for about an hour.

- **Appetite Suppression:** Sometimes, the body confuses thirst with hunger. Drinking water before meals can make you feel fuller, leading to reduced calorie intake.

- **Supports Exercise:** Adequate hydration ensures optimal performance during exercise. Being well-hydrated improves strength, power, and endurance, allowing you to work out more efficiently and burn more calories.

- **Removes By-products of Fat:** Water helps the body to get rid of waste. When you're burning fat for energy, water helps to transport the waste products out of the body.

How Much Water Should You Drink?

The amount of water you need depends on various factors, including your health, how active you are, and where you live. A general rule is to drink eight 8-ounce glasses of water a day, known as the "8x8 rule," which amounts to about 2 liters, or half a gallon. This is a reasonable goal for many people.

Tips for Staying Hydrated

- **Start Your Day with Water:** Begin each day by drinking a glass or two of water. It's a good way to wake up your body and get your system moving.

- **Use a Water Bottle:** Keep a refillable water bottle with you throughout the day. It serves as a constant reminder to drink up.

- **Eat Water-Rich Foods:** Fruits and vegetables like watermelon, cucumbers, oranges, and strawberries contain high amounts of water and can help you stay hydrated.

- **Set Reminders:** If you often forget to drink water, set reminders on your phone or computer at regular intervals.

Understanding the importance of hydration and implementing strategies to stay hydrated can significantly support your weight loss efforts.

Not only does it help with reducing appetite and increasing metabolism, but it also supports overall health, making your Chair Yoga practice and weight loss journey more effective.

9. Mindfulness and Meditation with Chair Yoga

Incorporating Mindfulness for Emotional Eating

Incorporating mindfulness into your daily life can be a transformative tool, especially in combating emotional eating.

Emotional eating is the act of using food as a way to suppress or soothe negative emotions, such as stress, anger, fear, boredom, sadness, and loneliness.

Major life events or, more commonly, the hassles of daily life can trigger negative emotions that lead to emotional eating and disrupt your weight loss efforts.

Mindfulness helps by bringing your attention to the present moment, making it easier to recognize and cope with the emotions and triggers that lead to emotional eating.

Understanding Mindfulness

Mindfulness is the practice of intentionally focusing on the present moment, accepting it without judgment. It's about acknowledging your thoughts, feelings, bodily sensations, and surrounding environment through a gentle, nurturing lens.

Strategies to Combat Emotional Eating with Mindfulness:

- **Mindful Eating:** Before eating, ask yourself why you're eating. Are you truly hungry, or are you trying to fill an emotional void? Mindful eating involves paying full attention to the experience of eating and drinking, both inside and outside the body. Notice the colors, smells, textures, and flavors of your food. Chew slowly and get rid of distractions like TV or reading.

- **Emotion Recognition:** Recognize the emotion you're feeling and name it. Simply saying, "I feel stressed," can help you understand and accept your emotions without judgment. Recognizing your feelings reduces the urge to consume food mindlessly.

- **Mindful Breathing:** When you feel the urge to eat due to emotions, take a few mindful breaths. Focus solely on your breathing—how the air feels entering and leaving your body. This can help pause the automatic response to reach for food.

- **Gratitude Journal:** Keeping a gratitude journal can shift your focus from negative emotions that lead to emotional eating to positive ones. Each day, write down three things you're grateful for. This practice can enhance mindfulness and provide a broader perspective on life.

- **Guided Imagery:** Use guided imagery to visualize a place that makes you feel calm and happy. This practice can help shift your focus away from food and reduce the intensity of your emotional triggers.

Incorporating mindfulness for emotional eating involves observing your patterns, triggers, and habits without judgment.

Chair Yoga can be a valuable part of this process, as it encourages a mindfulness practice through focused movement and breathing techniques.

By integrating these mindfulness strategies into your routine, you can gain a deeper understanding of your eating habits, learn to manage emotional triggers healthily, and support your weight loss journey.

Meditation Techniques for Stress Reduction and Focus

Meditation is a powerful practice for stress reduction and improving focus, key components in your Chair Yoga journey.

By incorporating meditation techniques, you can enhance your mental clarity, reduce anxiety, and create a sense of calm that supports both your physical yoga practice and your overall weight loss goals.

Introduction to Meditation Techniques

- **Focused Attention Meditation:** This involves concentrating on a single point of focus, such as your breath, a specific word, or a mantra. The aim is to gently bring your attention back whenever your mind wanders. This practice enhances your ability to concentrate and stay present.

- **Mindfulness Meditation:** This technique encourages you to observe wandering thoughts as they drift through your mind. The intention is not to get involved with the thoughts or judge them but simply to be aware of each moment. This form of meditation helps you become more aware of your thoughts and feelings related to eating and body image.

- **Body Scan Meditation:** Starting at one end of your body and moving through to the other, pay attention to each part of your body in turn. Notice any discomfort, tension, or sensations you feel. This practice helps connect your mind with your body, making you more attuned to your body's hunger and fullness signals.

- **Loving-Kindness Meditation:** Focus on developing feelings of goodwill, kindness, and warmth towards yourself and others. This can be particularly helpful in addressing the self-criticism and negative self-talk that often accompany weight loss efforts.

- **Visualization:** Create a detailed mental image of a peaceful place or situation. This technique can help reduce stress by focusing your mind on calming thoughts, diverting it from the stressors of daily life.

Incorporating Meditation into Your Chair Yoga Practice

To integrate these meditation techniques into your Chair Yoga practice, consider starting or ending each session with a few minutes of meditation. This can help prepare your mind and body for the physical practice, or it can help consolidate the calmness and focus achieved during your yoga session.

Additionally, setting aside specific times for meditation outside of your yoga practice can reinforce the benefits of stress reduction and improved focus in your daily life.

Even just a few minutes a day can make a significant difference in managing stress, reducing emotional eating, and supporting your weight loss journey.

Tips for Effective Meditation

1. **Start Small:** Begin with just a few minutes each day and gradually increase the time as you become more comfortable with the practice.

2. **Create a Routine:** Try to meditate at the same time each day to establish a habit.

3. **Find a Quiet Space:** Choose a peaceful place where you can relax without interruption.

4. **Be Patient:** Meditation is a skill that develops over time, so be gentle with yourself as you learn to quiet your mind.

By incorporating meditation techniques into your Chair Yoga routine, you can enjoy enhanced mental well-being, reduced stress, and a focused mind, all of which support a successful weight loss journey.

10. Lifestyle Adjustments for Long-Term Success

Creating a Sustainable Routine Beyond Chair Yoga

Creating a sustainable routine beyond Chair Yoga involves integrating habits and activities that support your overall health and weight loss goals in the long term.

The key is to find a balance that fits your lifestyle, preferences, and capabilities, ensuring that these practices are enjoyable and thus more likely to be maintained over time.

Steps to Creating a Sustainable Routine

1. **Set Realistic Goals:** Begin by setting achievable goals that motivate you without overwhelming you. These can range from small daily objectives to larger, long-term aspirations.

2. **Incorporate Variety:** To keep your routine engaging and prevent boredom, include a variety of exercises and activities. This could mean trying different styles of yoga, exploring other forms of low-impact exercises like swimming or walking, or even taking up a new hobby that encourages physical activity.

3. **Listen to Your Body:** Pay attention to how your body responds to different activities and adjust accordingly. It's essential to challenge yourself, but not to the point of strain or injury.

4. **Make It Social:** Engaging in physical activities with friends or family can increase your motivation and enjoyment. Whether it's attending a class together, going for walks, or simply practicing yoga at home with a companion, social interaction can enhance your commitment to a healthy lifestyle.

5. **Schedule Your Activities:** Just as you would with any important appointment, schedule your exercise and activity times. This helps in prioritizing your health and ensures that you make time for physical activity in your daily routine.

6. **Find Your "Why":** Identify and remind yourself of the reasons you started your chair yoga and physical activity journey. Whether it's for health reasons, to reduce stress, or to feel more energized, keeping your motivations in mind can help you stay on track.

Beyond Physical Activity

A sustainable routine isn't just about physical exercise. It also involves making mindful choices about your diet, ensuring you get enough sleep, managing stress, and fostering positive relationships.

These elements all contribute to a holistic approach to health and well-being that supports your chair yoga practice and weight loss goals.

Embrace Flexibility and Kindness

It's important to be flexible and kind to yourself as you establish and adjust your routine.

Life happens, and there will be days when you might not be able to stick to your plan. Instead of seeing this as a failure, view it as an opportunity to be adaptable and to listen to what your body and mind need at that moment.

Creating a sustainable routine beyond Chair Yoga is about building a lifestyle that supports your physical, mental, and emotional health. It's a journey of discovery, learning, and growth that can lead to profound changes in your well-being and quality of life.

Incorporating Physical Activity into Your Daily Life

Incorporating physical activity into your daily life is a cornerstone of maintaining your health and supporting the weight loss and wellness benefits gained from your Chair Yoga practice.

Physical activity doesn't have to mean spending hours at the gym or engaging in strenuous workouts. Instead, it's about finding opportunities to move more throughout your day in ways that are enjoyable and sustainable for you.

Steps to Incorporate Physical Activity

1. **Start Small:** If you're not used to regular physical activity, start with small, manageable actions. This could be as simple as taking a 5-minute walk around your home or office or doing a set of stretches during a break.

2. **Use Technology to Your Advantage:** There are numerous apps and online platforms offering short, guided exercise sessions, from walking to strength training, that you can do anywhere.

3. **Make It a Habit:** Try to make physical activity a regular part of your routine. Schedule it just like any other important activity. Consistency is key to forming new habits.

4. **Incorporate Movement into Daily Tasks:** Look for ways to be more active in your daily tasks. Take the stairs instead of the elevator, walk or cycle for short errands instead of driving, or do some gardening or house cleaning

5. **Stand More:** Standing burns more calories than sitting and can contribute to muscle tone and overall health. Consider a standing desk or take short standing or walking breaks if you have a desk job.

6. **Engage in Fun Activities:** Physical activity should be enjoyable. Dance to your favorite music, play with your children or pets, or join a recreational sports team. When you enjoy what you're doing, it doesn't feel like a chore.

Benefits of Daily Physical Activity

- **Improved Cardiovascular Health:** Regular movement helps strengthen the heart and improve circulation.

- **Enhanced Mood and Mental Health:** Physical activity releases endorphins, which have mood-boosting properties.

- **Increased Energy Levels:** Regular activity can boost stamina and reduce feelings of fatigue.

- **Better Sleep:** Being active during the day can help you fall asleep more easily and improve sleep quality.

- **Weight Management:** Alongside a balanced diet, physical activity is crucial for weight management and can help prevent weight gain.

Incorporating physical activity into your daily life is about making intentional choices to move more. It's not about overhauling your life overnight but gradually adopting more active habits that contribute to your overall well-being. Remember, every bit of movement counts, and the goal is to find what works best for you and what you can maintain over the long term.

11. YOUR BONUS

Exclusive Access to Video Tutorials

With the purchase of this book, you gain exclusive access to our comprehensive video library, a valuable tool designed to enhance your Chair Yoga practice. This visual resource provides step-by-step video tutorials for each exercise detailed in the book, allowing you to see the movements in action and follow along in real-time. Here's how to make the most of this feature:

Scan the QR code found below or enter this link: **bit.ly/chair-yoga-bonus** into your search browser.

Using the Video Library

1. **Browse by Chapter:** The video library is organized according to the book's chapters, making it easy to find the tutorial corresponding to the exercise you're reading about.

2. **Watch and Learn:** Each video demonstrates the correct technique for performing the exercises, with cues on alignment and breathing. Watch the videos before attempting the exercises to get a clear understanding of each movement.

3. **Practice Alongside:** Once you're familiar with the exercise, you can practice alongside the video, pausing or replaying sections as needed for clarification.

Enhancing Your Practice

- **Visual Learning:** For many, seeing an exercise performed is far more informative than reading about it. Use the videos to bridge the gap between theory and practice.

- **Self-Paced Learning:** With access to these tutorials, you can learn at your own pace, revisiting any exercise until you feel comfortable with its execution.

Staying Motivated

- **Track Your Progress:** Use the videos as a benchmark for progress. Over time, you'll notice improvements in your ability to follow along and execute the movements with precision.

- **Mix and Match:** Feel free to explore and mix exercises from different chapters to keep your routine varied and engaging.

The video library is a dynamic complement to your Chair Yoga journey, designed to support your learning and enhance your practice. Remember, consistent practice is key to reaping the full benefits of Chair Yoga, and these tutorials are here to guide you every step of the way.

Conclusion

The Journey Ahead

As you stand on the threshold of completing this book, it's essential to reflect on the journey you've embarked upon with Chair Yoga for weight loss.

The path ahead is filled with endless possibilities, and your commitment to integrating Chair Yoga into your daily routine marks the beginning of a transformative journey towards better health, enhanced flexibility, and a deeper connection with your body.

Embracing the Journey

- **Continued Practice:** The true essence of yoga lies in consistency. Continue to practice the poses, flows, and breathing techniques you've learned, allowing them to evolve as you grow stronger and more flexible.

- **Exploration:** Don't hesitate to explore new poses or sequences. Chair Yoga offers a safe foundation to experiment and discover what works best for your body and goals.

- **Holistic Approach:** Remember, weight loss and wellness go beyond physical exercises. Incorporate the nutritional guidelines and mindfulness practices introduced in this book to support your overall health journey.

Beyond the Book

- **Community:** Join online forums, social media groups, or local classes to connect with others on similar paths. Sharing experiences and challenges can provide motivation and a sense of belonging.

- **Lifelong Learning:** Yoga is a journey of lifelong learning. Consider advancing your practice by exploring other forms of yoga or deepening your understanding of Chair Yoga through workshops and courses.

- **Self-Reflection:** Regularly take time to reflect on your progress. Celebrate your achievements, no matter how small, and set new goals to continue your journey of self-improvement.

The Impact of Your Practice

The benefits of Chair Yoga extend far beyond weight loss. As you incorporate these practices into your life, you'll likely notice improvements in your mental clarity, emotional resilience, and overall well-being. Chair Yoga teaches us to meet our bodies where they are, offering a path to wellness that is accessible and empowering.

Final Thoughts

The end of this book is not the end of your journey but a new beginning. With the foundation you've built, you're well-equipped to continue exploring the vast world of yoga and wellness. Remember, every pose you master, every mindful breath you take, is a step towards a healthier, happier you. Embrace the journey ahead with an open heart and an eager spirit, and let Chair Yoga be your guide to a life filled with balance, strength, and peace.

Your Voice Matters

As you reflect on the insights and progress you've made through this Chair Yoga journey, we kindly ask you to share your experience. Leaving a positive review not only supports our work but also helps others discover the transformative power of Chair Yoga for weight loss and well-being. Your feedback is invaluable, offering insights, inspiration, and encouragement to both us as authors and to fellow readers embarking on their own paths to health and happiness.

How to Leave a Review:

- **Visit Amazon**

- **Share Your Thoughts:** Click on the option to write a review. Don't worry about making it perfect; just speak from the heart.

- **Impact:** By sharing your journey, challenges you've overcome, and the benefits you've experienced, you can profoundly impact someone else's life.

Your review not only celebrates your achievements but also lights the way for others to follow in your footsteps towards a healthier, more balanced life. We are deeply grateful for your support and for choosing to share your journey with us. Thank you for considering leaving a positive review and for being an essential part of our Chair Yoga community.

Together, we can inspire a movement towards wellness that transcends the pages of this book.

Thank you for joining us on this Chair Yoga journey. Your commitment to improving your health and well-being is truly inspiring.
Remember, each breath, stretch, and moment of mindfulness moves you closer to the balance and vitality you deserve. It's been a privilege to accompany you on this path.

Barbara Lewiss